THEY PIERCED THE VEIL

... and Saw the Future

By J. R. Church

All scripture references are from the King James Version unless otherwise stated.

They Pierced the Veil ... and Saw the Future

First Edition, 1993

Copyright © 1993 by J. R. Church

Printed in the United States of America

Published by:

Prophecy Publications

P. O. Box 7000

Oklahoma City, OK 73153

Library of Congress Catalog Card Number 93-083181

ISBN 0-941241-12-2

Dedicated to . . .

All who love to study the Prophets

Foreword

The Minor Prophets pierced the veil of time and saw the future. In fact, their descriptions of the twentieth century are somewhat uncanny. Since the restoration of Israel in 1948, the messages of these twelve men have taken on a new and powerful dimension of prophetic fulfillment.

Yet, this set of Old Testament prophets have been largely overlooked by Christian theologians. Unfortunately, since they are called the Minor Prophets, they seem to have been automatically relegated to a minor position of importance.

For example, the redemption of Hosea's wayward wife may be viewed as a prophetic metaphor for modern Israel. Joel's plague of locusts may correspond to the advancing army in Revelation 9. The metaphors of the lion and bear in the books of Hosea and Amos appear to be descriptive of Great Britain and Russia. These fascinating metaphors appear over and over. Their themes are cohesive—the restoration of Israel and judgment of the nations in the *"day of the Lord."*

In the first century, the twelve Minor Prophets were compiled together as one book. Only in later years did Christian theologians divide them into separate writings.

These twelve short writings by early Jewish prophets were so similar in content and design, it seems only right that they should be considered together. Furthermore, because of their treatment of prophetic events destined for fulfillment in the *"day of the Lord,"* I felt the need to emphasize the prophetic nature of these Minor Prophets.

This work is, by no means, a thorough study of the lives and times of these prophets. My intention is to encourage you to take a fresh look at their collective prophetic message. I think you will find that it has a consistent theme which describes the times in which we live.

This book will take you on a journey through the Minor Prophets and show you what they predicted for the concluding years of the sixth and the introductory years of the seventh millennia.

Table of Contents

According to Peter's translation of Joel's prophecy, this *"early"* and *"latter rain"* will come in the *"last days."* This was spoken by the same man who wrote in II Peter 3:8 that *"one day is with the Lord as a thousand years and a thousand years as one day."*

Using the plural term *"last days,"* I think Peter could have been referring to these 2,000 years since Calvary and Pentecost. When the Holy Spirit was poured out on the Day of Pentecost, He represented the beginning of Joel's prophecy concerning the *"last days"*— indicating at least **two** days or 2,000 years. What began with the Spirit of God being poured out upon all flesh 2,000 years ago will end according to Joel's description:

"... I will show wonders in heaven above, and signs in the earth beneath; blood and fire and vapour of smoke:

"The sun shall be turned into darkness, and the moon into blood, before that great and notable day of the Lord come ..." (Joel 2:19-20).

The significant thing about Joel's prophecy is that he described both the beginning and the ending of this dispensation. Obviously, the sun did not turn into darkness nor the moon into blood on that day when the Holy Spirit empowered the early church. In fact, it has been almost 2,000 years now and the sun has not yet turned into darkness nor the moon into blood. The prophecy still awaits fulfillment.

The Captivity of Judah

Joel explained the key ingredient which will introduce the end of this dispensation and the introduction of the latter rain:

> *"For, behold, in those days, and in that time, when I shall bring again the captivity of Judah and Jerusalem"* (Joel 3:1).

This is a prophecy of the return of the Jews to the land of Israel which began to be fulfilled in 1948. With the return of the Jew to his land, God is preparing for that most devastating war of history:

> *"Proclaim ye this among the Gentiles; Prepare war, wake up the mighty men, let all the men of war draw near; let them come up:*
>
> *"Beat your plowshares into swords, and your pruninghooks into spears ..."*
>
> *"Multitudes, multitudes in the valley of decision: for the day of the Lord is near in the valley of decision"* (Joel 3:9-10,14).

What a dreadful description—when the armies of an unbelieving world reject the love of an offended God and the message goes out to the Gentiles, *"Prepare war."* Then Jesus Christ will return to gain the victory! What a description!—written by the prophet Joel.

Chapter Three

Amos
The Burdenbearer

Though Amos, whose name means "burden-bearer," is listed as third among the twelve Minor Prophets of the Old Testament, his predictions are among the most relevant for the 20th century.

You may recall in our study of Hosea that a certain group of animals were used to describe nations in the latter days. Hosea used the symbol of the lion, the leopard, and the bear. Well, in like manner, Amos spoke of these animals as metaphors of events that would come to pass in the *"day of the Lord:"*

> *"Woe unto you that desire the **day of the Lord!** to what end is it for you? the **day of the Lord** is darkness, and not light.*
>
> *"As if a man did flee from a **lion**, and a **bear** met him; or went into the house, and leaned his hand on the wall, and a **serpent** bit him"* (Amos 5:18-19).

Like Hosea before him, Amos, whose writings appeared about the same time as Hosea's, also used the symbols of the lion and bear. It seems that some of his contemporaries were ex-

cited about the prospects for the day of the
Lord. They felt it might be a wonderful occasion. Amos, on the other hand, chided them for
their enthusiasm and declared that the day of
the Lord will bring judgment. He said, *"Woe
unto you that desire the day of the Lord!"* It will
not be a time of peace, but war. It will not be a
time of light, but darkness. There will be no joy,
only sorrow. That was the message of Amos.

The Lion and Bear

Amos said it will be *"as if a man did flee
from a lion, and a bear met him."* In other
words, there will be no escape. Everywhere the
Jewish people turn they will find sorrow and
woe. I believe it is a description of this generation, for the lion could represent Great Britain,
and the bear may represent Russia.

Great Britain became the possessor of
Palestine under the mandate of the so-called
Balfour Declaration, which promised the land
to the Jews. However, once the British took
possession, they reneged on their promise and
tried to keep the Jews from coming back home
to the land of their forefathers. In 1947 the
Jewish people literally had to fight the British
to gain possession of their homeland. Thus, we
have Israel's conflict with the lion.

However, at the next turn Israel must face
the bear—which many are convinced will represent a Russian horde. One of these days
Russia will invade Israel. It is written in the

Bible, and all of the politicians in Washington and all of the statesmen in Europe will not be able to stave off that future bloody conflict. But the verse does not end there. After the man *"fled from a lion, and a bear,"* Amos said he then went into *"the house, leaned his hand on the wall and a serpent bit him."*

The house, in my opinion, represents the house of the Lord—the rebuilding of a Jewish sanctuary on the Temple site in Jerusalem.

Inside the house of the Lord, the serpent (a symbol of the antichrist) will bite the hand of the Jew. To me, that is a prophecy of the "abomination of desolation." One of these days the Jewish people will erect a sanctuary on the Temple site. Amos gave us a magnificent description of it in the last chapter of his book, in verses 11-12:

> *"In that day will I raise up the tabernacle of David that is fallen, and close up the breaches thereof; and I will raise up his ruins, and I will build it as in the days of old:*
>
> *"That they may possess the remnant of Edom, and of all the heathen, which are called by my name, saith the Lord that doeth this"* (Amos 9:11-12).

Yes, Amos is the prophet who specifically predicted that the Tabernacle of David will be restored in Jerusalem, and that in the house of the Lord the nation of Israel will receive the symbolic serpent's bite. The serpent was an ancient symbol for the tribe of Dan, predicted producer of the antichrist. In fact, the symbol of the serpent takes us all the way back to the eagle. That does not mean that the antichrist will come from the United States. We must remember that the symbol of the German Empire was an eagle. Under that symbol, six million Jews were killed during the days of World War II. Furthermore, the symbol of both the Imperial Roman Empire and the Holy Roman Empire was an eagle.

The Final Judgment

Obadiah describes that great final cataclysmic judgment poured out by an offended God when he wrote:

> *"For the day of the Lord is near upon all the heathen: as thou hast done, it shall be done unto thee: thy reward shall return upon thine own head.*
>
> *"For as ye have drunk upon my holy mountain, so shall all the heathen drink continually, yea, they shall drink, and they shall swallow down, and they shall be as though they had not been.*
>
> *"But upon mount Zion shall be deliverance, and there shall be holiness; and the house of Jacob shall possess their possessions"* (Obadiah 15-17).

Finally, Obadiah predicts that the land of Edom will become the possession of the house of Israel. When the antichrist commits the "abomination of desolation" in the middle of the Tribulation Period, 144,000 Jews will flee to the mountain stronghold of Petra for safety.

In that day, the situation will be reversed. The antichrist will possess Jerusalem and the children of Israel will possess Petra. While Israel is cared for in the wilderness of Edom, a rumor from the Lord will create confusion between the antichrist and his allies.

It may be that just as the Ammonites and Moabites turned against their former friends, the Edomites, even so the former allies of the antichrist may turn against him in the battle of Armageddon. In the midst of that battle, Jesus Christ will appear to gain the victory over those warring nations. He will establish the promised kingdom and rule for a thousand years.

Chapter Five

Jonah
The Dove

The book of Jonah is considered to be the earliest of the Minor Prophets (C. I. Scofield suggested the date of 862 B.C.). Yet it holds the fifth position among the twelve. Furthermore, the book does not contain a single prophecy in the ordinary sense. The only *"thus saith the Lord"* in the entire book is Jonah's prediction that Nineveh would be overthrown in 40 days— and, of course, his prediction turned out to be wrong. Yet, it is obvious that the book has a tremendous prophetic story to tell.

These four chapters give not only the story of Jonah's encounter with a great fish, but also provides a prophetic scenario for the nation of Israel. It is a prophecy set forth in the form of a parable, giving the story of Jonah's rebellion against the call of God to take the message of His judgment and justice to the Gentiles.

Jonah headed in the other direction, but could not escape the unusual plan of God for his life. After spending three days in the stomach of a great fish, he was ready to make his journey across the Fertile Crescent and preach a great revival in Nineveh, the capital city of the Assyrian empire.

Jonah's Background

I might say, Jonah was a respected prophet in the ninth century B.C. In II Kings 14 we are told of a prediction made by Jonah which came true during the reign of Jeroboam, the king of Israel:

> *"He restored the coast of Israel from the entering of Hamath unto the sea of the plain, according to the word of the Lord God of Israel, which he spake by the hand of his servant Jonah, the son of Amittai, the prophet, which was of Gath-hepher" (II Kings 14:25).*

We are told that the Lord saw the affliction of the Jewish people and declared that He would not blot out the name of Israel from under heaven. He promised to save them by the hand of Jeroboam, who restored and secured the northern borders of Israel, recovering Damascus and Hamath, which had belonged to Judah. It was Jonah who predicted the restoration of Israel's northern border.

Jonah was not always wrong in his predictions. In fact, he was not altogether wrong when he declared to Nineveh that God would destroy the city in 40 days. Just because God did not destroy the city at the end of 40 days does not mean that Jonah was not accurate. It simply means that when a sinful people repent and seek the forgiveness of God, the Heavenly

Another early historian, Diodorus Siculus, referred to Nahum's prophecy:

"There was an old prophecy that Nineveh should not be taken until the river became an enemy to the city. And in the third year of the siege, the river being swollen with continual rains, overflowed every part of the city, and broke down the wall for 20 furlongs; then the king, thinking that the oracle was fulfilled, and the river become an enemy to the city, built a large funeral pile in the palace, and collecting together all his wealth and his concubines and eunuchs, burnt himself and the palace with them all; and the enemy entered at the breach that the waters had made and took the city."

The old prophecy that Nineveh should not be taken until the river became an enemy to the city must have been by the pen of Nahum, who wrote these words about 40 years before the fall of Nineveh. According to the historian who described the battle scene, we learn that the king himself was aware of the prophecy of Nahum and committed suicide rather than face the Babylonian army.

It is interesting to note that a flood accompanied the destruction of Nineveh. The flood became a metaphor for war. Some day, either another flood or war will bring about the destruction of antichrist and his system of world government. Psalm 93:3 says:

"The **floods** have lifted up, O LORD, the **floods** have lifted up their voice; the **floods** lift up their waves" (Psalm 93:3).

Early Jewish theologians wrote that of those three floods, the first represented the Babylonian destruction of Jerusalem, the second referred to the Roman destruction of the Temple, and the third pointed toward the future battle of Gog and Magog.

Daniel also used the metaphor of a flood when he wrote in Daniel 9:26:

> *"... and the end thereof shall be with a **flood**, and unto the end of the war desolations are determined"* (Daniel 9:26).

Again in chapter 11, verse 22, Daniel described the time of the antichrist:

> *"And with the arms of a **flood** shall they be overflown from before him, and shall be broken ..."* (Daniel 11:22).

Furthermore, our Savior made a reference to that future flood. He said:

> *"As it was in the days of Noah, so shall it be also in the days of the Son of man"* (Luke 17:26).

Nahum was right on target. He predicted not only the destruction of Nineveh, but the future judgment of that mystery city, Babylon the Great.

Just as Nineveh had destroyed other cities, so shall Nineveh be destroyed. Thebes, the ancient capital of upper Egypt was destroyed by the Assyrians in 666 B.C. Nahum called it, "No." The modern name is Luxor:

"And it shall come to pass, that all they that look upon thee shall flee from thee, and say, Nineveh is laid waste: who will bemoan her? whence shall I seek comforters for thee?

"Art thou better than populous No, that was situate among the rivers, that had the waters round about it, whose rampart was the sea, and her wall was from the sea?

"Ethiopia and Egypt were her strength, and it was infinite; Put and Lubim were thy helpers.

"Yet was she carried away, she went into captivity ..." (Nahum 3:7-10).

In these verses, Nahum declares that Nineveh is no better off that the Egyptian city she destroyed. He was saying that as Nineveh destroyed Thebes (or No), so will Nineveh be destroyed.

Then Nahum concludes his prophecy by saying:

"There is no healing of thy bruise; thy wound is grievous: all that hear the bruit [news] of thee shall clap the hands over thee: for upon whom hath not thy wickedness passed continually" (Nahum 3:19).

"There is no healing," wrote Nahum, only the awesome destruction of God's judgment upon a wicked world system.

And when the news of her destruction is given, the saved of all the ages will clap their hands and rejoice. We will be glad that the old serpent is destroyed and the King of glory sits upon His throne forever—and to know Him is life eternal!

Chapter 8

Habakkuk
The Wrestler

Not much is known of the life of Habakkuk in the Old Testament. We are not told who he was or when he lived. Yet, he is regarded as one of the inspired prophets of Israel's ancient past. The rabbis pronounce his name as "Ha'-ba-kook'," meaning "the wrestler." Jewish tradition claims he was from the tribe of Simeon and was a contemporary of Jeremiah. He is said to have remained in the land along with Jeremiah when the Babylonians carried his people into captivity.

The form of the book is that of a dialogue between Habakkuk and the Lord. His name befits the occasion. Habakkuk wrestled with the dilemma befalling his nation. The prophet could not understand why God would bring such a wicked nation as the Chaldeans to destroy the sacred city and carry away captive the Chosen People. The first four verses give the prophet's complaint, followed immediately by the Lord's answer. The dialogue continues in this manner throughout the book.

In chapter 2, the Lord goes far beyond the

prophet's thoughts and previews the final dispensation of human history—when Christ will come to set up the long-looked-for kingdom.

Chapter 3 concludes with a prayer by Habakkuk. It is one of the most moving portions of Old Testament Scripture.

While the primary interpretation of the book concerns Israel and Babylon during those dark days following the captivity, it nevertheless contains both practical applications for the Dispensation of Grace, and prophetic implications concerning the Second Coming of Christ.

The Prophet's Complaint

As the book opens, we find Habakkuk complaining to the Lord—perhaps during the initial Babylonian invasion of Jerusalem.

He was highly disturbed that God would allow the wicked and corrupt Chaldeans to conquer a people who were not nearly so wicked as they. Here's the way he put it in verses 1-4:

"The burden which Habakkuk the prophet did see.

"O Lord, how long shall I cry, and thou wilt not hear! even cry out unto thee of violence, and thou wilt not save!

"Why dost thou shew me iniquity, and cause me to behold grievance? for spoiling and violence are before me: and there are that raise up strife and contention.

"Therefore the law is slacked, and judgment doth never go forth: for the wicked doth compass about the righteous; therefore wrong judgment proceedeth" (Habakkuk 1:1-4).

Oh, was he ever upset! Though he had what appears to be a legitimate question, he was quite presumptuous to demand an answer from God. I would not suggest that the average person attempt such a complaint.

Who are we to argue with our great Creator? If one is to wrestle with the Lord and get away with it, then he must be one who walks with God. The Lord could have taken his breath away without a moment's notice. God could have stopped the beat of his heart in an instant—and yet, He did not.

God is angered by the sin of a rebellious people, but is kind and gracious at the complaints of His children. You may recall that Jonah was punished for disobeying the call of God. Yet, at the end of his book, when Jonah complained that God did not punish Nineveh as He had proposed, God did not punish Jonah for his complaint.

Also, from his prison cell, John the Baptist complained that Jesus did not come to his rescue, saying, *"Are you really the Christ, or do we look for another?"* The disciples marveled at his impudence. Yet, Jesus corrected them saying, *"No greater man was ever born of woman than John."* Yes, even John's complaint did not provoke the anger of God. And here Habakkuk questions God's motive for allowing a far more wicked and perverse people to conquer the beloved city of Jerusalem and carry its people away captive.

The Lord's Answer

Observe the following verse as the Lord spoke:

"Behold ye among the heathen, and regard, and wonder marvelously ..." (Habakkuk 1:5a).

I can imagine God was saying, "Look, Habakkuk, I have sent the Chosen People to live among the heathen for a reason. The captivity is not a historical mistake. Though the Chaldeans are more wicked, I have raised them up to punish my wayward people." Here, I think, God was saying, "Habakkuk, lift up your eyes and look beyond the immediate. Look into the far future. Understand that the difficulties which have befallen the Jewish people, though not now understood, will result in a far greater blessing in the future." And then He said in the last half of the fifth verse:

"... for I will work a work in your days, which ye will not believe, though it be told you" (Habakkuk 1:5b).

In this verse, I think God is saying, "The Babylonian captivity is just the beginning of a history filled with dispersions as I send the Jewish people among the nations of the world—not only in the sixth century B.C., but for the next 2500 years." Why? So that God can work a work so marvelous that the Jewish people will not believe it even though it is told to them. God was driving the Jewish people from their land so that He could call:

"And it shall come to pass, that every one that is left of all the nations which came against Jerusalem shall even go up from year to year to worship the King, the Lord of hosts, and to keep the feast of tabernacles."

Thus, we come to that Blessed Hope which is the message of every prophet throughout the Bible. One day the kingdom of heaven will be established on this earth and Christ will reign as King of kings and Lord of lords.

At that time, the Feast of Tabernacles, which has been a prophetic picture of the future kingdom, will be observed from year to year.

Chapter 12

Malachi
My Messenger

Through the pages of this book we have reviewed the lives and works of the Minor Prophets and have considered their messages in the light of this generation. The twelfth and last of these prophets was Malachi, who wrote his book around 396 B.C., toward the end of Nehemiah's rule in Jerusalem. Of the man himself we know little, only that his name means *"my messenger."*

After his message was completed, there were no more writing prophets. His book represents not only the last of the twelve Minor Prophets, but the last book of the Old Testament as well. After Malachi, there were 400 years of silence wherein the Jewish people had no word from God. Such a spiritual drought was foreseen, however, in the message of Malachi.

His book, made up of only four chapters, begins in the days of a corrupt priesthood which, over the years, developed into the two major divisions of the Pharisees and the Sadducees along with a few other splinter groups.

The Controversy

One of the most important features of the book is the controversy between God and His people. Again and again the Lord charged them with spiritual apostasy, departing in their hearts from the one whom they outwardly professed to serve. And each time, the priesthood dared to contradict God's testimony of their calloused condition. It is Phariseeism at its worst, claiming to serve God outwardly while inwardly corrupt.

1. The Love of God

The controversy between the Lord and His Pharisaic priesthood began on a tender note. The priesthood were reminded that God loved them:

> *"I have loved you, saith the Lord ..."* (Malachi 1:2a).

In spite of God's display of compassion, the priesthood seemed convinced that God did not love them and that the Lord delighted in punishing the Jewish people:

> *"... Yet ye say, Wherein hast thou loved us?"* (Malachi 1:2b).

This prevailing attitude reminds me of a bitterness which prevails in this generation. During the days of World War II, it was said that some among the Jewish people cried, "Oh

God, if we are the Chosen People, please choose somebody else for a while." As it was in the days of Malachi, so it is today. The Jewish people have spurned the love of God, blaming Him for all their troubles.

2. The Sins of the Priesthood

As the controversy continued, the Lord reminded them:

> *"A son honoreth his father, and a servant his master: if then I be a father, where is mine honour? and if I be a master, where is my fear? saith the Lord of hosts unto you, O priests, that despise my name. And ye say, Wherein have we despised thy name?"* (Malachi 1:6).

By grace, God chose the offspring of Jacob over Esau's descendants, and yet the Jacobites did not show respect for the Sovereign of the universe. When told that they are despisers of His name, they retorted quite callously, *"Wherein have we despised thy name?"*

Solemnly, He brought their sins before them, declaring that polluted bread was offered on His altar, only to have another sarcastic question thrown at him:

> *"... Wherein have we polluted thee?"* (Malachi 1:7).

The patience and grace of God is distinctly clear at this point. The Jewish priesthood does not appear to be interested in having an intimate relationship with God. Though they served Him in Nehemiah's newly rebuilt

Temple, their hearts are far from Him. Kindly, God reminded them that they considered the table of the Lord to be contemptible. They offered the blind, the lame, and the sick in sacrifice and had kept the best for themselves. Would they dare to offer the lame to the leader of their land? No. Then why should they offer the blind and the sick to God? Malachi pleaded with the priesthood:

"And now, I pray you, beseech God that he will be gracious unto us ..." (Malachi 1:9).

And yet the priesthood refused to repent and accept the grace of God, thinking that they had done no wrong. The priesthood had become so calloused that they demanded to be paid for every bit of religious service they performed. They would not even shut the doors at night without wages. They would not even kindle the fire upon the altar except they demanded wages for it, and God was saying, "Your heart is not in your work. I'd just as soon you would not do anything for Me if you are going to act that way about it."

Concerning their service to the Lord, they said:

"Behold what a weariness it is!" (Malachi 1:13).

That was the attitude of the religious leaders during Malachi's day, as well as the people. Malachi reminded them that they had departed from the covenant made with Levi:

"But ye are departed out of the way; ye have caused many to stumble at the law; ye have corrupted the covenant of Levi, saith the Lord of hosts.

"Therefore have I also made you contemptible and base before all the people, according as ye have not kept my ways, but have been partial in the law" (Malachi 2:8-9).

What an indictment against the priesthood who were charged with maintaining the spiritual condition of the people!

III. The Sins of the People

At this point, a spiritual indictment was made against those followers of the priesthood, the common people:

"Have we not all one father? hath not one God created us? why do we deal treacherously every man against his brother, by profaning the covenant of our fathers?" (Malachi 2:10).

As go the priests, so go the people. God had no alternative but to bring His indictment against them. The Lord put it this way:

"Judah hath dealt treacherously, and an abomination is committed in Israel and in Jerusalem; for Judah hath profaned the holiness of the Lord which he loved, and hath married the daughter of a strange god" (Malachi 2:11).

What an indictment! The Jewish people had not kept their vows, yet they could not see it. They retorted with the question:

"Wherefore? (Malachi 2:14).